Australian Animals
Crocodiles

by Lyn A. Sirota

Consulting Editor: Gail Saunders-Smith, PhD

Content Consultant: Dr. Mike Letnic
Research Fellow, School of Biological Sciences
University of Sydney, Australia

CAPSTONE PRESS
a capstone imprint

Pebble Plus is published by Capstone Press,
151 Good Counsel Drive, P.O. Box 669, Mankato, Minnesota 56002.
www.capstonepress.com

092009
005618CGS10

Books published by Capstone Press are manufactured with paper
containing at least 10 percent post-consumer waste.

Library of Congress Cataloging-in-Publication Data
Sirota, Lyn A., 1963-
    Crocodiles / by Lyn A. Sirota.
    p. cm. — (Pebble plus. Australian animals)
    Includes bibliographical references and index.
    Summary: "Simple text and photographs present crocodiles, their physical features, where they live, and what
they do" — Provided by publisher.
    ISBN 978-1-4296-4504-1 (library binding)
    1. Crocodiles — Juvenile literature. I. Title. II. Series.
QL666.C925S57 2010
597.98'2 — dc22   2009040492

Editorial Credits
Gillia Olson, editor; Bobbie Nuytten, designer; Wanda Winch, media researcher; Eric Manske, production specialist

Photo Credits
Ardea/David Hancock, 17
Corbis/Theo Allofs, cover
Nature Picture Library/Michael Pitts, 21
Shutterstock/Ashley Whitworth, 5; John Austin, 11; Neale Cousland, 15; Susan Flashman, 1, 13
www.marinethemes.com/Kelvin Aitken, 7, 9, 19

Note to Parents and Teachers

The Australian Animals set supports national science standards related to life science. This
book describes and illustrates crocodiles. The images support early readers in understanding
the text. The repetition of words and phrases helps early readers learn new words. This book
also introduces early readers to subject-specific vocabulary words, which are defined in the
Glossary section. Early readers may need assistance to read some words and to use the Table of
Contents, Glossary, Read More, Internet Sites, and Index sections of the book.

Table of Contents

Living in Australia

Australia is home to two kinds
of toothy crocodiles.
One is the freshwater crocodile.
It lives in freshwater rivers
and streams.

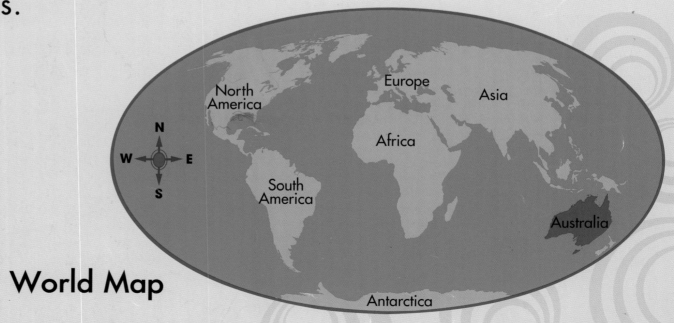

World Map

The saltwater crocodile
also lives in Australia.
It lives in freshwater rivers.
But it also lives in salt water
where rivers meet the ocean.

Australia
Map

where crocodiles live

Up Close!

Crocodiles are long reptiles. Saltwater crocodiles grow up to 17 feet (5.2 meters) long. Freshwater crocodiles grow up to 9 feet (2.7 meters) long.

Crocodiles have big mouths.
More than 60 sharp teeth
fit in their mouths.
Their teeth may break off,
but they grow back quickly.

A crocodile's body
is covered with scales.
Hard bony plates
under the scales
make ridges on their backs.

Master Predators

Crocodiles are predators.

They wait for their prey

to come near.

Only the croc's eyes and

nostrils poke out of the water.

Snap!

Crocodiles will eat any animal

in or near the water.

Fish, frogs, and kangaroos

may all be crocodile meals.

Life Cycle

Female crocodiles lay between
five and 70 eggs at one time.
Babies hatch in about 90 days.
Their mother takes them
to the water.

Staying Safe

Mother crocodiles stay
with their young
for several weeks or months.
Mothers protect their young
from danger.

Glossary

freshwater — water that does not have salt; most ponds, rivers, lakes, and streams have fresh water.

nostril — an opening in an animal's nose used for breathing

plate — a flat, bony growth

predator — an animal that hunts other animals for food

prey — an animal hunted by another animal for food

reptile — a cold-blooded animal that breathes air and has a backbone; most reptiles lay eggs and have scaly skin.

salt water — water that is salty; salt water is found in oceans.

scale — one of the small pieces of hard skin that cover the body of a fish or reptile

Read More

Buckingham, Suzanne. *Meet the Crocodile.* Scales and Tails. New York: PowerKids Press, 2009.

Kaufman, Gabriel. *Saltwater Crocodile: The World's Biggest Reptile.* SuperSized! New York: Bearport, 2007.

Tourville, Amanda Doering. *A Crocodile Grows Up.* Wild Animals. Minneapolis: Picture Window, 2007.

Internet Sites

FactHound offers a safe, fun way to find Internet sites related to this book. All of the sites on FactHound have been researched by our staff.

Here's all you do:

Visit *www.facthound.com*

FactHound will fetch the best sites for you!

Index

Word Count: 193
Grade: 1
Early-Intervention Level: 20